# Contents

# How to use this book

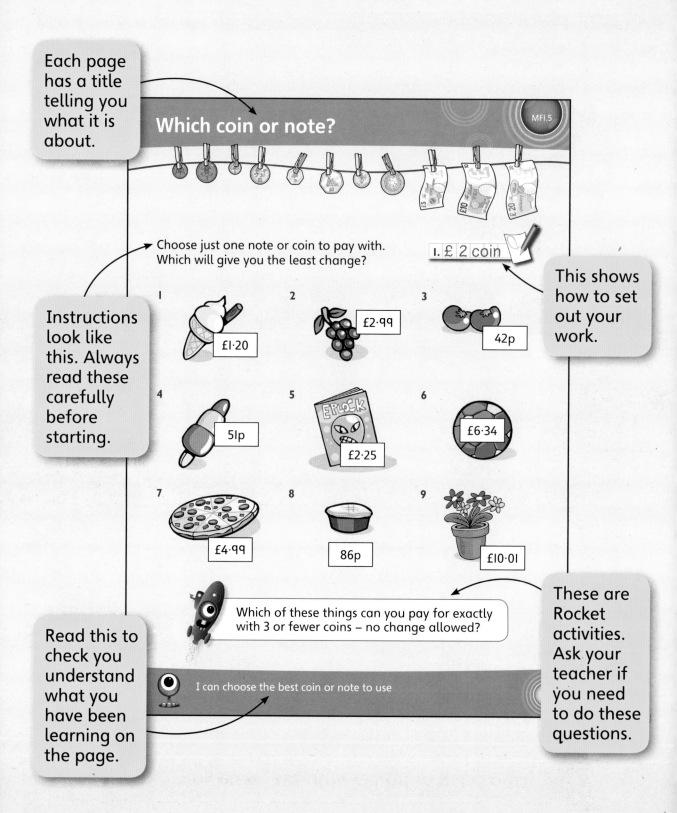

Each page has a title telling you what it is about.

## Which coin or note?

MFI.5

Choose just one note or coin to pay with. Which will give you the least change?

This shows how to set out your work.

1. £2 coin

Instructions look like this. Always read these carefully before starting.

1 £1·20

2 £2·99

3 42p

4 51p

5 £2·25

6 £6·34

7 £4·99

8 86p

9 £10·01

Which of these things can you pay for exactly with 3 or fewer coins – no change allowed?

These are Rocket activities. Ask your teacher if you need to do these questions.

Read this to check you understand what you have been learning on the page.

I can choose the best coin or note to use

2

# Same values

Write the total value of the coins in each purse.

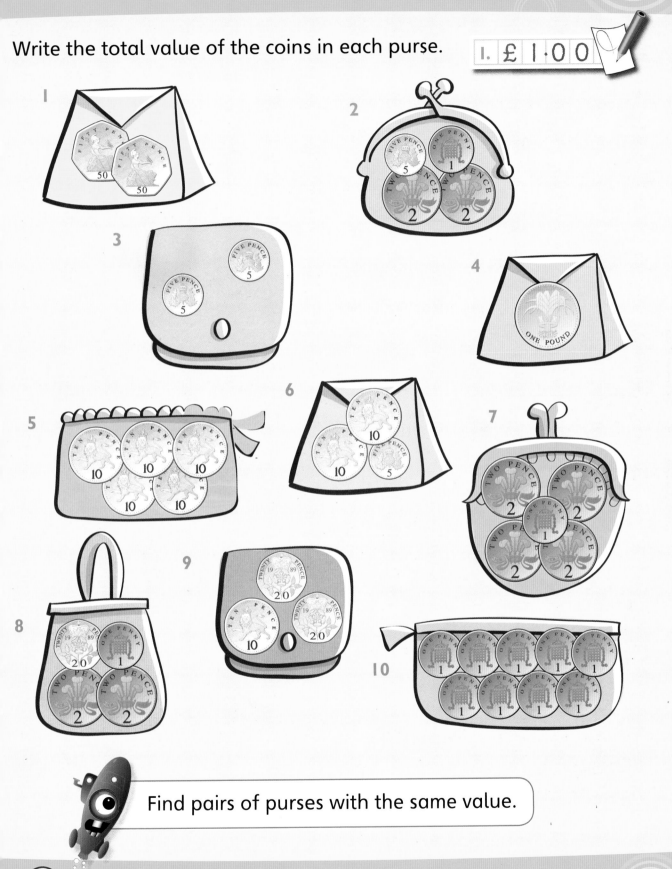

1. £1·00

Find pairs of purses with the same value.

I can find the total of a set of coins

# Totals

Write the amount in each till.

1. £ | 1 | 5

1
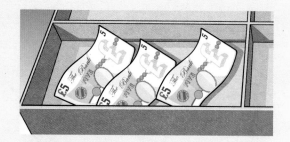

2

3

4

Write the amount in each purse.

5. £ | 1 | · | 2 | 4

5
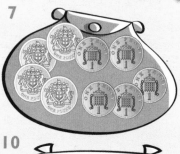

6
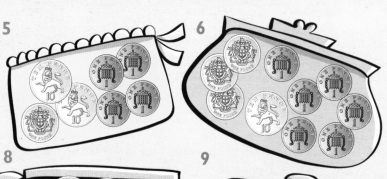

7

8

9

10

What amounts can you make using £1 and one other coin? How about £2 and another coin?

I can find the total of a set of coins and notes

# How much?

People put sets of coins into the vending machine.
Write the total of each set of coins.

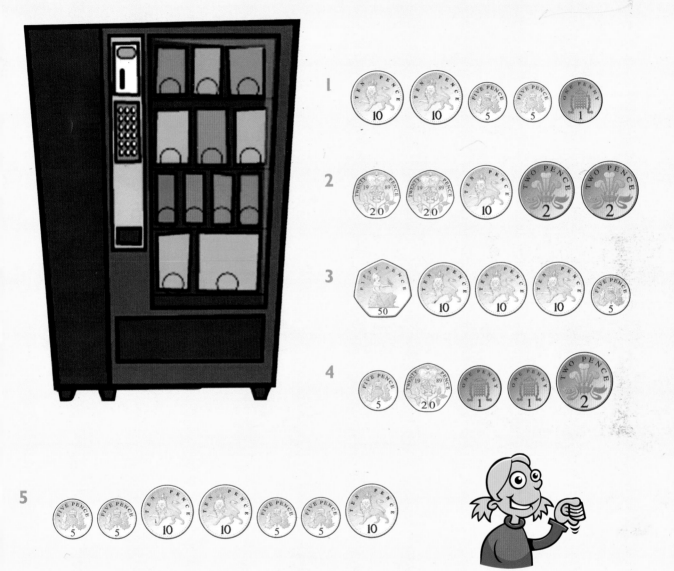

1   10  10  5  5  1

2   20  20  10  2  2

3   50  10  10  10  5

4   5  20  1  1  2

5   5  5  10  10  5  5  10

6   2  2  2  5  2  5  2  5

7   Which of the coins would you use to pay for something
costing 58p?

I can find the total of a set of coins

5

# Fewest coins

Write which coins you would use to pay for each item. Use the fewest coins you can.

1. 5p and 2p

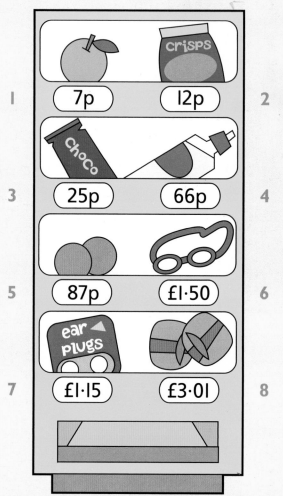

1   7p          12p   2

3   25p         66p   4

5   87p         £1·50 6

7   £1·15       £3·01 8

9   Use as few coins as you can to buy items 5 and 8 together.

Draw a vending machine like this, with items for sale. The machine only takes £1, 20p and 5p coins so price the items carefully.

 I can choose the fewest coins to pay

# True or false?

Write true or false for each statement.

1   Ten 5p coins have the same value as five 10p coins.

2   Two £10 notes have the same value as ten 20p coins.

3   Ten £5 notes have the same value as ten 5p coins.

4   Five £1 coins have the same value as ten 50p coins.

5   Twenty 20p coins have the same value as two £2 coins.

Write two true and two false statements like these.

   I can exchange coins and notes for others with the same value

7

# Which is cheaper?

Write which is cheaper and by how much.

1. b is cheaper by 35p

1  a  75p   b  40p

2  a  48p   b  51p

3  a  78p   b  65p

4  a  64p   b  49p

5  a  87p   b  £1

6  a  85p   b  £1·10

7  a  £1·50   b  £1·05

8  a  98p   b  £1·99

Find the difference between the cheapest and most expensive item on this page.

# Can I afford it?

Is there enough money in the purse to pay for the cake? Write yes or no.

1. no

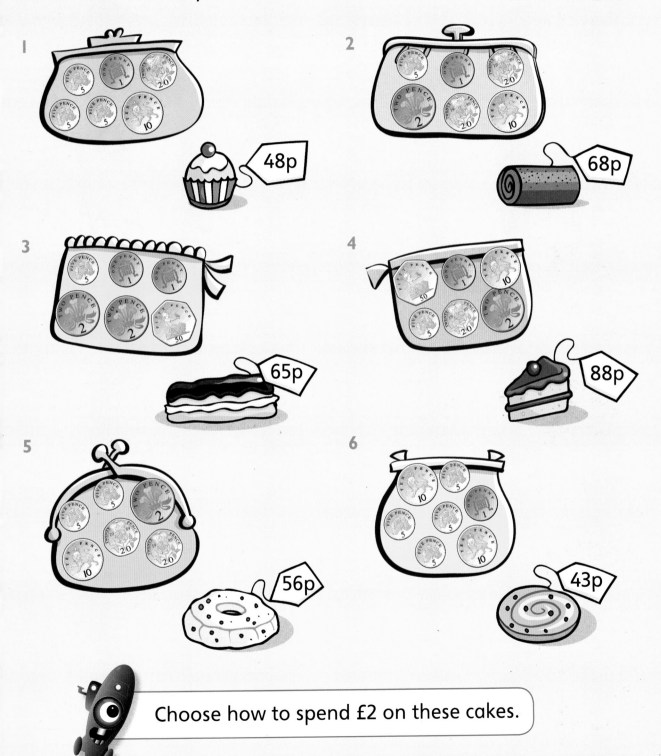

1

48p

2

68p

3

65p

4

88p

5

56p

6

43p

Choose how to spend £2 on these cakes.

I can compare how much I have with the cost of items

# Prices

1 Write the prices in order from the cheapest to the most expensive.

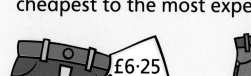

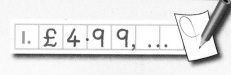

1. £ 4 . 9 9 , ...

£6·25

£5·05

£12·50

£8·40

£4·99

£9·49

£8·04

£9·99

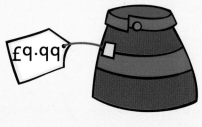

£11·99

2 Draw three T-shirts with price labels. They are more expensive than the red top but cheaper than the pink shirt. Choose different prices to write on the labels.

3 How many of the items above cost between £9·50 and £12?

Look in a clothes catalogue and choose how to spend £50.

I can compare and order written amounts of money

# Which coin or note?

Choose just one note or coin to pay with.
Which will give you the least change?

 1. £2 coin

**1**

£1·20

**2**

£2·99

**3**

42p

**4**

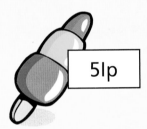

51p

**5**

EPLOCK

£2·25

**6**

£6·34

**7**

£4·99

**8**

86p

**9**

£10·01

 Which of these things can you pay for exactly with 3 or fewer coins – no change allowed?

I can choose the best coin or note to use

# Can I afford them?

Is there enough money in each purse to pay for the items? Write yes or no.

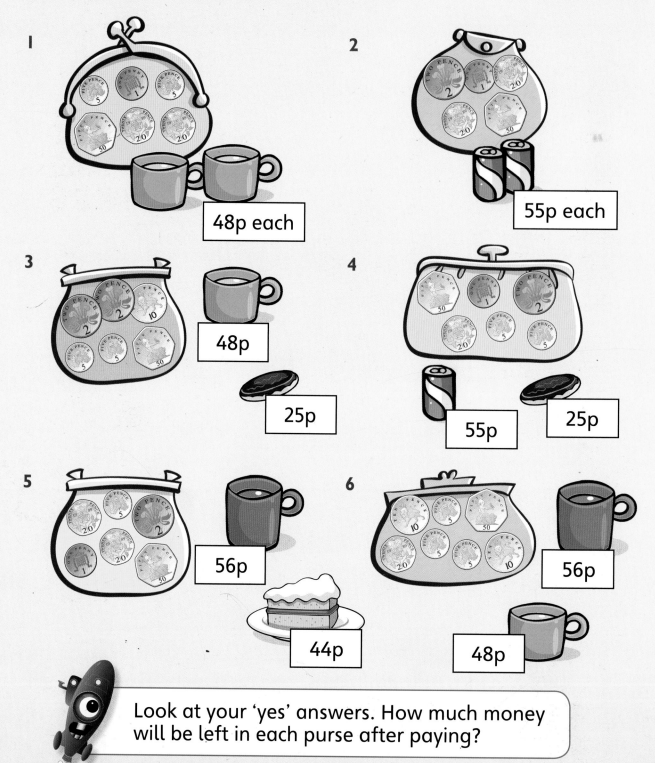

**1**

48p each

**2**

55p each

**3**

48p

25p

**4**

55p

25p

**5**

56p

44p

**6**

56p

48p

Look at your 'yes' answers. How much money will be left in each purse after paying?

I can find the cost of items and say if they are affordable

# Money problems

**1** Choose three items. Add the prices. Write the total in £ and pence. Do this six times.

| | 8 | 5 |
| - | - | - |
| | 4 | 4 |
| | 7 | 6 |
| 2 | 0 | 5 | p |
| £ 2 · 0 5 | | |

85p

39p

13p

54p

76p

62p

95p

APPLE PIE

44p

28p

67p

**2** What coins will pay for each item? Use as few as possible. No change allowed!

| 8 | 5 | p |
| - | - | - |
| 1 × | 5 0 | p |
| 1 × | 2 0 | p |
| 1 × | 1 0 | p |
| 1 × | 5 | p |

**3** Jenny has four silver coins.
List four amounts she could have.
Which is the most? Which is the least?

Make up a problem like this for your partner to do.

I can solve money problems

13

# Money problems

How much to buy each pair of items?

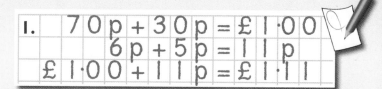

$$1. \quad 70p + 30p = £1·00$$
$$6p + 5p = 11p$$
$$£1·00 + 11p = £1·11$$

**1**

35p    76p

**2**

25p    47p

**3**

17p    65p

**4**

45p    78p

**5**

75p    58p

**6**

56p    74p

**7**

84p    75p

**8**

£1·35    61p

**9**

34p    £1·20

Add 78p to each money box. How much is in there now?

**10**

45p

**11**

88p

**12**

60p

**13**

68p

Add 66p to each purse. How much is in there now?

**14**

85p

**15**

59p

**16**

£1·68

**17**

£1·75

A pizza and a drink come to £1·71. They each cost less than £1. What could the prices be? Write 5 answers.

I can find totals

# How much for one?

The total cost of the ice-creams is shown. Find the cost of one.

1. $69p ÷ 3 = 23p$ each

**1**

total cost = 69p

**2**

total cost = 88p

**3**

total cost = £1·10

**4**

total cost = 93p

**5**

total cost = £1·28

**6**

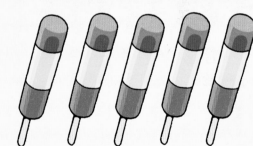

total cost = £2·50

Make up a problem like this about 5 ice-creams. What total costs would work? Try some and see.

I can find the price of one when given the price of several

15

# Sharing

Each group of children put their money together and then share it equally. How much will each child get?

1.  27p   15p   18p

2.  54p   24p   12p

3.  14p   29p   27p   18p

4.  21p   21p   12p   10p   26p

5.  32p   £1   18p

6.  £1   £2   £5   40p

7.  55p   £1·20   £1·05   £2

8.  1p   £1   £1   10p   £3·04

Make up another question like this for your partner to solve. Make sure the children can get equal amounts.

I can find totals and share totals equally

# Special offers

There is a Buy One Get One Free offer.
Write how much each item costs you, if you buy two.

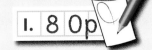
I. 8 0p

**1**  £1·60

**2**  £2·80

**3**  £3·10

**4** SOAP 76p

There is a Buy Two Get the Third Free offer.
Write how much each item costs you, if you buy three.

5. 2 0p

**5**  30p

**6**  £1·50

**7**  90p

**8**  £1·20

> Make up a problem like this for your partner to do. Make sure you know the answer!

# Ticket prices

The box shows the ticket prices for a theme park.

1 How much will these two pay?

ADULT **£12**

CHILD **HALF THE ADULT PRICE**

SENIORS **(OVER 65s) £4 OFF THE ADULT PRICE**

**\* \* \* \***

SPECIAL OFFER! **SPEND OVER £50 AND GET A £5 DISCOUNT**

2 Grandma is 70. How much will they pay?

3 Grandpa is 55. How much will this family pay?

4 How much will this family pay?

5 Both grandparents are 70. How much will this family pay?

Work out how much your family would pay.

I can solve money problems

18

# Special offers

There is a Buy One Get One Half Price offer. Write how much you pay if you buy two of each item.

1. £18 + £9 = £27

**1**  £18

**2**  £3·20

**3**  £25

**4**  £5·90

**5**  £2·80

**6**  £4·20

**7**  £7·20

**8**  £36

 Make up a problem like this for your partner to do. Make sure you know the answer!

I can work out how much to pay for items in special offers

# Block graphs

The graph shows what colour counters are in the bag.

**Colours of counters**

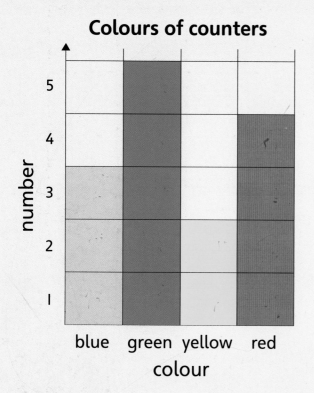

Use the graph to write the number of:

1   red counters

2   blue counters

3   yellow counters

4   green counters

5   blue and green counters

6   green and yellow counters

7   blue and red counters

8   green and red counters

9   counters altogether

10   counters that are not red

Find 20 counters in any colour. Make your own block graph to show how many you have in each colour. Hide some counters then ask your partner to look at your graph and say which colour counters you have hidden.

I can answer questions about simple block graphs

# Pictograms

**Number of ice-creams sold**

| | | | | | | |
|---|---|---|---|---|---|---|
| strawberry | 🍦 | 🍦 | 🍦 | 🍦 | | |
| vanilla | 🍦 | 🍦 | 🍦 | 🍦 | 🍦 | |
| mint | 🍦 | 🍦 | | | | |
| chocolate | 🍦 | 🍦 | 🍦 | 🍦 | 🍦 | 🍦 |

 means I ice-cream

Write the number of ice-creams sold that are:

I    mint

2    strawberry

3    chocolate

4    vanilla

5    mint or chocolate

6    vanilla or strawberry

7    Write the number of ice-creams sold altogether.

 Ice-creams cost 50p each. How much does the ice-cream man get for the strawberry ice-creams he has sold? For the vanilla ice-creams? For all the ice-creams?

 I can answer questions about simple pictograms

# Pictograms

I  Draw your own pictogram, like the one that has been started, to show the colours of the boats.

**Boat colours**

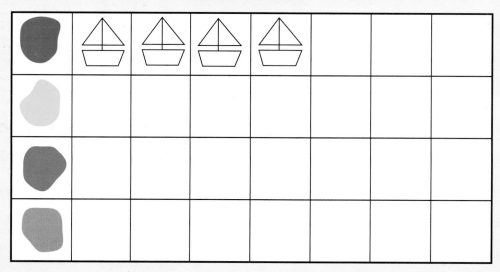

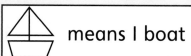 means I boat

Make up some questions about the pictogram for your partner to answer.

 I can draw my own pictogram

# Venn diagrams

1  Copy the Venn diagram. Make sure you draw it
   big enough! Write each name in the correct place.

Gita    Chuy

Amit    Tom

Raj     May

Bella   Debbie

Zoe     Paul

Ann     John

Mick    Natalie

fewer than 4 letters        not fewer than
                                4 letters

Children's  names

2  Copy the Venn diagram. Think of more words to write on it.

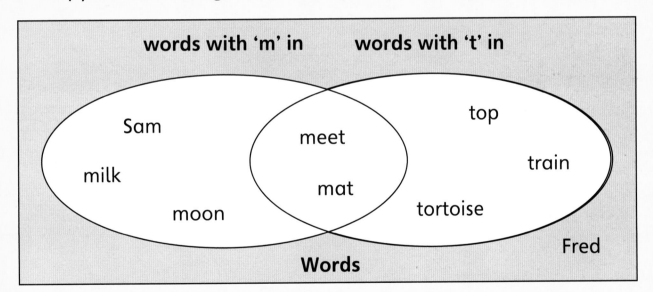

words with 'm' in        words with 't' in

Sam

milk

moon

meet

mat

top

train

tortoise

Fred

Words

Draw a Venn diagram to show something about
your toys, for example 'with wheels' or 'no wheels'.

I can sort information onto a Venn diagram

23

# Carroll diagrams

1  Look at the Carroll diagram. Put the words in the correct sections.

|  | Joining word | Not joining word |
|---|---|---|
| Short word (fewer than 4 letters) |  |  |
| Not short word (4 or more letters) |  |  |

cat

where

but

table

dog

chair    and    which    because

2  Use a book to find more words. Write them on the diagram.

What could the column and row headings be on this Carroll diagram?

|  |  |  |
|---|---|---|
|  | remote-control car | doll teddy |
|  | TV computer | bike pogo stick |

I can sort information onto a Carroll diagram

# Carroll and Venn diagrams

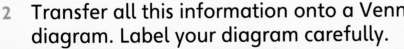

1 Copy the Carroll diagram. Write the words that should go in each section. Think of other words to write on the diagram.

|  | 2 syllables or fewer | Not 2 syllables or fewer |
|---|---|---|
| Words rhyming with sea |  |  |
| Words not rhyming with sea |  |  |

summery

autumn

tree

wasp

wispy

beautiful

blustery

cheerfully

spring

imagining

wind

bee

free

sun

2 Transfer all this information onto a Venn diagram. Label your diagram carefully.

Copy the empty Carroll diagram above. Open a book and look at the first 20 words. If you sort them onto the diagram, which section do you think will have the most words in? Now sort them. Were you right?

I can sort information onto Venn and Carroll diagrams

# Carroll and Venn diagrams

1  Look at the Venn diagram. Draw a Carroll diagram to show the same information.

2  Add another 10 animals to both diagrams.

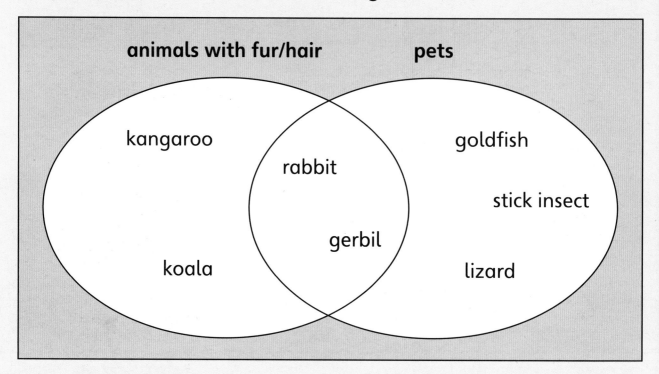

**animals with fur/hair**        **pets**

kangaroo

rabbit

goldfish

stick insect

gerbil

koala        lizard

3  Sort the numbers between 20 and 50 onto this diagram.

|  | Multiples of 3 | Not multiples of 3 |
|---|---|---|
| Odd |  |  |
| Not odd |  |  |

Look at the Carroll diagram. Change 'Multiples of 3' and 'Not multiples of 3' to another multiple so that one section on the diagram is empty.

I can sort information onto Venn and Carroll diagrams

# Always, sometimes, never

Say whether each statement is:
always true; sometimes true; never true.

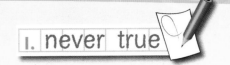

1  The day after Sunday is Tuesday.

**November**

| Mon | Tue | Wed | Thu | Fri | Sat | Sun |
|-----|-----|-----|-----|-----|-----|-----|
| 1 | 2 | 3 | 4 | 5 | 6 | 7 |
| 8 | 9 | 10 | 11 | 12 | 13 | 14 |
| 15 | 16 | 17 | 18 | 19 | 20 | 21 |
| 22 | 23 | 24 | 25 | 26 | 27 | 28 |
| 29 | 30 | | | | | |

2  The day after Wednesday is Thursday.

3  An hour has 60 minutes.

4  A month has 30 days.

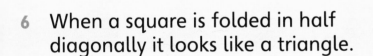

5  When a triangle is folded in half
   it looks like a square.

6  When a square is folded in half
   diagonally it looks like a triangle.

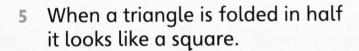

7  A year has 365 days.

3 + 5

1 + 7        15 + 1

9 + 11

8  The total of two odd numbers is even.

Make up some statements and ask your
partner to say whether they are: always
true; sometimes true; never true.

I can say whether something is always, sometimes or never true

27

# Likelihood

Say whether each event is:
impossible; unlikely; likely to happen.

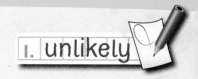
I. unlikely

1 Someone in your family will win the lottery.

2 You will see a car today.

3 It will rain tomorrow.

4 You will go to the moon this week.

5 Someone in your class will be away tomorrow.

6 Your teacher will sing a song tomorrow.

7 You will meet a crocodile on your way to school tomorrow.

8 It will snow this week.

Write an event that is:

9 likely          10 unlikely          11 impossible

I can say how likely something is to happen

# Likelihood

Say whether each event is impossible;
unlikely; likely to happen.

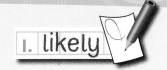

1  I will eat dinner today.

2  I will eat chips tonight.

3  One day I will go to America.

4  Tomorrow I will go to school.

5  The next person I see will be a boy.

6  Next year I will learn to swim.

7  Next week I will be younger.

8  One day I will be rich.

9  One day I will be married.

10  I will fall over tomorrow.

Think up 10 impossible events.

 I can say how likely something is to happen

# Likelihood

Draw a table like this. Decide how likely each event is and write the number in the correct column of the table.

| likely | unlikely | impossible |
|--------|----------|------------|
|        |          | 1          |

1  I will land on Mars tonight.

2  I will go to bed late tonight.

3  I will walk more than 10 steps today.

4  I will find a four-leaf clover today.

5  I will watch television tonight.

Draw a table like this. Decide how often each event happens and write the number in the correct column of the table.

| always | sometimes | never |
|--------|-----------|-------|
|        |           |       |

6  I go to sleep at night.

7  The moon shines in my window.

8  I have sweet dreams.

9  I wake up and get up.

10  I take the tiger for a walk.

11  I eat ice-cream for breakfast.

Make up more statements for each column of your two tables.

I can say how likely something is to happen

# Pictograms

Look at the pictogram. Answer the questions.

 means 2

| Where people in Class X live | |
|---|---|
| bungalow |  |
| terraced house | |
| semi-detached house | |
| detached house | |
| block of flats | |

1 How many people live in a terraced house?

2 What is the most common type of housing?

3 How many people do not live in a detached house?

4 How many people were asked about their house?

Draw your own table about people in your class.

# Pictograms

Ramon drew a pictogram showing the colours of cars driving down the street.

 means 2

| Colours of cars I saw | | | | | | |
|---|---|---|---|---|---|---|
| | | |  | | | |
| | | | |  | | |
| | | | | | | |
| | | | | | | |
| | | | | | | |
| | | | | | | |
| blue cars | black cars | white cars | green cars | red cars | yellow cars | purple cars |

1 How many blue cars?

2 How many cars were red?

3 How many cars were either black or white?

4 Which was the most common colour?

5 Which was the least common colour?

6 Which was the second most common colour?

7 How many cars were red, blue, green or yellow?

What other things could you look at in a traffic survey?

I can answer questions about simple pictograms

# Pictograms

1   Use the results in the tally chart to draw a pictogram.
    Use a smiley face to represent **two** children.

| Equipment people use | Number of children |
|---|---|
| CD player | ⪼ ⪼ ⫽⫽⫽⫽ |
| mobile phone | ⪼ ⫽⫽⫽ |
| television | ⪼ ⪼ |
| video player | ⪼ |
| DVD player | ⪼ ⫽⫽ |
| portable music player | ⪼ ⫽ |

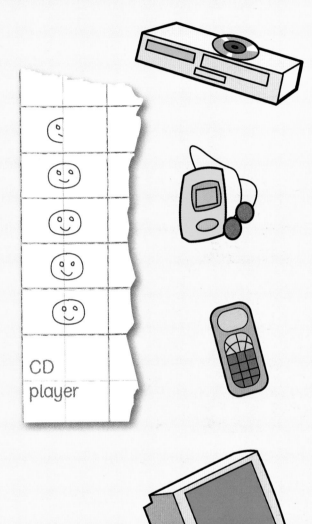

CD player

2   How many children use a mobile phone?

3   How many more children use a DVD player
    than use a video player?

Can you think of four more categories
to add? Talk to your partner.

# Bar graphs

Study the bar graph. Answer the questions.

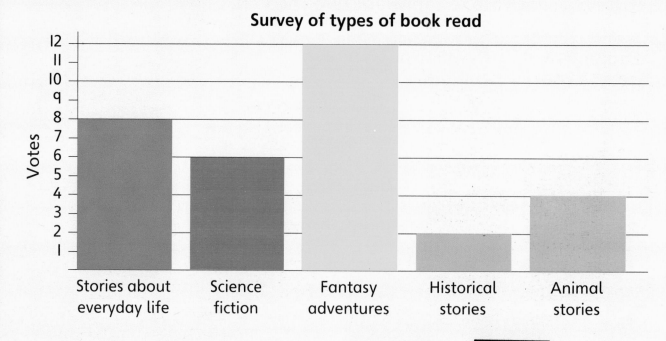

**Survey of types of book read**

Which type of story is:

1 most popular?
2 least popular?
3 liked by 8 children?

How many children:

4 like the most popular story type?
5 like animal stories?
6 like animal stories or science fiction?

Suppose each child had just one vote.
How many children were asked to vote?
What if each child had two votes?

# Bar graphs

Look at the bar graph. Answer the questions.

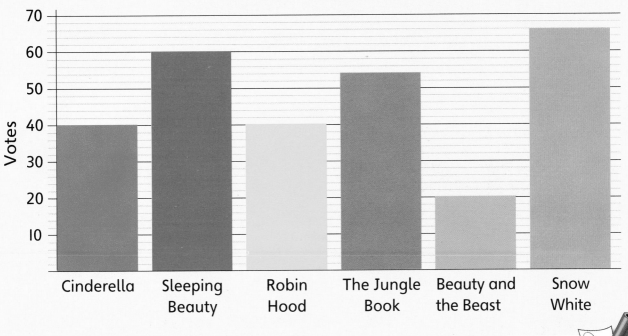

**Favourite films in Willowtree School**

1. 5 4

1  How many children like The Jungle Book?

2  Which two films are liked by the same number of children?

3  Which film is the most popular?

4  Which film is the least popular?

5  How many children like Robin Hood?

6  How many more children like Sleeping Beauty than like Beauty and the Beast?

Carry out your own film survey, using your friends' opinions.

I can answer questions about simple bar graphs

# Questionnaires

Work with your partner. Choose a question to find out about. Write a questionnaire or recording sheet.

> Is it true that more children in our class have birthdays in winter than summer?

or

> Which is the most common type of shoe fastening in school: laces, Velcro®, elastic or buckles?

or

> Is it true that the children in our school would prefer to have a shorter lunchtime and go home earlier?

or

> Which do the children in our class choose as their favourite lesson?

Think about...
Are the questions clear?
What might the answers be?
Do you need to suggest answers for people to choose from?
Have you got enough space for recording the information?
Is the sheet quick to fill in?

I can write my own questionnaire

# Questionnaires

Here are two questionnaires. One is a
much better questionnaire than the other.

1   Write at least five reasons why the second is better.

Do you eat bread?
Do you like it?
How often do you eat it?
How much do you eat?
Which type of bread do you prefer?

| | | Yes | No |
|---|---|---|---|
| 1 | Do you like bread? (If no, stop the survey now) | ☐ | ☐ |

| 2 | Which type of bread do you prefer? | Brown | ☐ |
|---|---|---|---|
| | | White | ☐ |
| | | Wholemeal | ☐ |

| 3 | How often do you eat bread? | Every day | ☐ |
|---|---|---|---|
| | | A few times a week | ☐ |
| | | Less than once a week | ☐ |
| | | Other ........................................... | |

| 4 | About how many slices of bread do you eat at: | | |
|---|---|---|---|
| | | Breakfast? | ☐ |
| | | Lunch? | ☐ |
| | | In the evening? | ☐ |

2   Write a questionnaire asking people about cooked potatoes,
    such as chips, mash, boiled or roasted ones.

I can say what is good or bad about a questionnaire

# Displaying information

1   Look around your classroom. Count the numbers of:

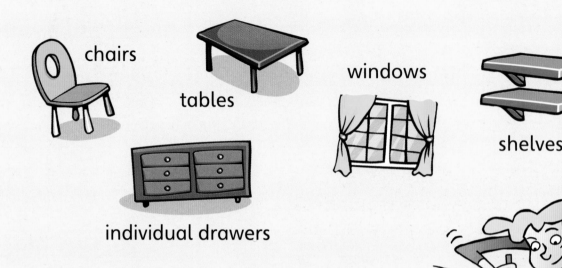

chairs

tables

windows

shelves

individual drawers

2   Draw a chart to show the information
    you collected about things in
    your classroom.

3   Find about 20 words in a dictionary,
    book or spelling list.

> Has at least
> two vowels

    Sort the words onto a Venn, Carroll
    or tree diagram. Use these labels
    on your diagram:

> Has two letters
> the same

4   Now sort the same words, using the same labels, but onto
    a different kind of diagram than you chose before.

> Talk to your partner about how the two
> sorting diagrams are alike or not alike.

  I can make decisions about how to display information

# Charts

1   Choose one question to find out about.

> What type of TV programme is most popular with children in the class?

or

> What do the children in our class say is their favourite type of fruit?

or

> Which season of the year do most children in our class have their birthday?

| Spring | Summer |
| Autumn | Winter |

or

> Which would the children in our class vote as their favourite pet?

2   Find out the answer by asking other children in your class. Record what you find.

3   Draw a chart or graph to show the information. Label it carefully and write a title.

I can collect information and draw my own chart

We would like to say a special thanks to all of the children who entered our design a character competition, and congratulations to our winners!

**WINNER**

Character designed by Tony Thomas, age 6,
St Helen's Primary School, Glasgow
Killer the Swordfish

Interpretation of the winning design by
Volker Beisler (professional illustrator)

Author Team:
Lynda Keith, Hilary Koll and Steve Mills

Published by Pearson Education Limited, Edinburgh Gate, Harlow, Essex, CM20 2JE.

www.pearsonschools.co.uk

Text © Pearson Education Limited 2011

Typeset by Debbie Oatley @ room9design
Illustrations © Harcourt Education Limited 2006-2007, Pearson Education Limited 2011
Illustrated by Piers Baker, John Haslam, Nigel Kitching, Mark Ruffle, Eric Smith, Andrew Hennessey, Gary Swift, Andy Hammond, Matt Buckley, Seb Burnett, Debbie Oatley, Jim Peacock, Dave Williams, Chris Winn, Anthony Rule, Annabel Tempest, Glen McBeth
Cover design by Pearson Education Limited
Cover illustration Volker Beisler © Pearson Education Limited
Printed in Malaysia, CTP-KHL

The authors Lynda Keith, Hilary Koll and Steve Mills assert their moral right to be identified as the authors of this work.

First published 2011

15 14 13 12
10 9 8 7 6 5 4 3

**British Library Cataloguing in Publication Data**
A catalogue record for this book is available from the British Library

ISBN 978 0 435 04786 3

**Acknowledgements**
Every effort has been made to contact copyright holders of material reproduced in this book.
Any omissions will be rectified in subsequent printings if notice is given to the publishers.